Silly Knock-
Jokes for Kids!

By Silly Billy

Knock, knock.

Who's there?

Orange.

Orange who?

Orange you going to let me in?

Knock, knock.

Who's there?

Canoe.

Canoe who?

Canoe help me with my homework?

Knock, knock.

Who's there?

Anee.

Anee, who?

Anee one you like!

Knock, knock.

Who's there?

Iva.

Iva who?

I've a sore hand from knocking!

Knock, knock.

Who's there?

Dozen.

Dozen who?

Dozen anybody want to let me in?

Knock, knock.

Who's there?

Henrietta.

Henrietta who?

Henrietta worm that was in his apple.

Knock, knock.

Who's there?

Avenue.

Avenue who?

Avenue knocked on this door before?

Knock, knock.

Who's there?

Harry.

Harry who?

Harry up, it's cold out here!

Knock, knock.

Who's there?

Adore.

Adore who?

Adore is between us. Open up!

Knock, knock.

Who's there?

King Tut.

King Tut who?

King Tut-key fried chicken!

Knock, knock.

Who's there?

Otto.

Otto who?

Otto know. I've got amnesia.

Knock, knock.

Who's there?

Otto.

Otto who?

Otto know what's taking you so long!

Knock, knock.

Who's there?

Merry.

Merry who?

Merry Christmas!

Knock, knock.

Who's there?

Noah.

Noah who?

Noah good place we can get something to eat?

Knock, knock.

Who's there?

Dwayne.

Dwayne who?

Dwayne the bathtub, It's overflowing!

Knock, knock.

Who's there?

Isabell.

Isabell who?

Is a bell working, I had to knock?

Knock, knock.

Who's there?

Tank.

Tank who?

Your welcome!

Knock, knock.

Who's there?

Watson.

Watson who?

What's on tv tonight?

Knock, knock.

Who's there?

Alex.

Alex who?

Alex-plain later!

Knock, knock.

Who's there?

Lettuce.

Lettuce who?

Lettuce in it's cold out here.

Knock, knock.

Who's there?

Annie.

Annie who?

Annie body home?

Knock, knock.

Who's there?

Cook.

Cook who?

Hey! Who are you calling cuckoo?

Knock, knock.

Who's there?

Ketchup.

Ketchup who?

Ketchup with me and I'll tell you!

Knock, knock.

Who's there?

Dishes.

Dishes who?

Dish is a nice place!

Knock, knock.

Who's there?

Spell.

Spell who?

W-H-O

Knock, knock.

Who's there?

Althea.

Althea who?

Althea later alligator!

Knock, knock.

Who's there?

Norma Lee.

Norma Lee who?

Norma Lee I don't go around knocking on doors, but I just had to meet you!

Knock, knock.

Who's there?

CD.

CD who?

CD guy on your doorstep?

Knock, knock.

Who's there?

Somebody.

Somebody who?

Somebody too short to ring the doorbell!

Knock, knock.

Who's there?

Witches.

Witches who?

Witches the way home?

Knock, knock.

Who's there?

Iowa.

Iowa who?

Iowa big apology to the owner of that red car!

Knock, knock.

Who's there?

Abbot.

Abbot who?

Abbot you don't know who this is!

Knock, knock.

Who's there?

Viper.

Viper who?

Viper nose, it's running!

Knock, knock.

Who's there?

Banana

Banana who?

Banana split!

Knock, knock.

Who's there?

Beets!

Beets who?

Beets me!

Knock, knock.

Who's there?

Beef

Beef who?

Before I get cold, you'd better let me in!

Knock, knock.

Who's there?

Olive

Olive who?

Olive right next door to you.

Knock, knock.

Who's there?

Turnip

Turnip who?

Turnip the volume, it's quiet in here.

Knock, knock.

Who's there?

Ice cream

Ice cream who?

Ice cream if you don't let me in!

Knock, knock.

Who's there?

Abe

Abe who?

Abe C D E F G H...

Knock, knock.

Who's there?

Doughnut!

Doughnut Who?

Doughnut ask, it's a secret!

Knock, knock.

Who's there?

Ada

Ada who?

Ada burger for lunch!

Knock, knock.

Who's there?

Alex.

Alex who?

Hey, Alex the questions around here!

Knock, knock.

Who's there?

Alma

Alma who?

Alma not going to tell you!

Knock, knock.

Who's there?

Amy

Amy who?

Amy fraid I've forgotten!

Knock, knock.

Who's There?

Anita

Anita who?

Anita to borrow a pencil!

Knock, knock.

Who's there?

Annie.

Annie who?

Annie body going to open the door already?

Knock, knock.

Who's there?

Ben.

Ben who?

Ben knocking for 20 minutes!

Knock, knock.

Who's there?

Claire.

Claire who?

Claire the way; I'm coming in!

Knock, knock.

Who's there?

Doris.

Doris who?

Doris locked. Open up!

Knock, knock.

Who's there?

Frank!

Frank who?

Frank you for being my friend!

Knock, knock.

Who's there?

Howard!

Howard who?

Howard I know?

Knock, knock.

Who's there?

Robin.

Robin who?

Robin the piggy bank again.

Knock, knock.

Who' s there?

Kent!

Kent who?

Kent you tell who I am by my voice?

Knock, knock.

Who's there?

Justin.

Justin who?

Justin the neighborhood and thought I'd come over.

Knock, knock.

Who's there?

Lena

Lena who?

Lena little closer and I'll tell you!

Knock, knock.

Who's there?

Ken

Ken who?

Ken I come in, it's freezing out here?

Knock, knock.

Who's there?

Nana.

Nana who?

Nana your business who's there.

Knock, knock.

Who's there?

Tyrone

Tyrone who?

Tyrone shoelaces!

Knock, knock.

Who's there?

Nobel

Nobel who?

No bell, that's why I knocked!

Knock, knock.

Who's there?

Sherlock.

Sherlock who?

You Sherlock your door up tight!

Knock, knock.

Who's there?

Wendy.

Wendy who?

Wendy bell works again I won't have to knock anymore.

Knock, knock.

Who's there?

Will

Will who?

Will you let me in? It's freezing out here!

Knock, knock.

Who's there?

Alpaca

Alpaca who?

Alpaca the trunk, you pack the suitcase!

Knock, knock.

Who's there?

Honey bee.

Honey bee who?

Honey bee a dear and get me some juice.

Knock, knock.

Who's there?

Monkey!

Monkey who?

Monkey see. Monkey do.

Knock, knock.

Who's there?

Who

Who who?

Is there an owl in here?

Knock, knock.

Who's there?

Amish!

Amish who?

Awe, I miss you too.

Knock, knock.

Who's there?

Atch!

Atch who?

Bless you!

Knock, knock.

Who's there?

Canoe!

Canoe who?

Canoe come out and play with me today?

Knock, knock.

Who's there?

Cash.

Cash who?

**No thanks, but I'll take a peanut if you have
one!**

Knock, knock.

Who's there?

Cargo!

Cargo who?

Car go beep, beep!

Knock, knock.

Who's there?

Dishes.

Dishes who?

Dishes a nice place you got here.

Knock, knock.

Who's there?

Broccoli!

Broccoli who?

Broccoli doesn't have a last name, silly.

Knock, knock.

Who's there?

Doctor.

Doctor who?

You've seen that TV show?

Knock, knock.

Who's there?

From.

From who?

Actually, grammatically speaking you should say "from whom."

Knock, knock.

Who's there?

Howl.

Howl who?

Howl you know it's really me unless you open the door?

Knock, knock.

Who's there?

Leaf

Leaf Who?

Leaf Me Alone!

Knock, knock.

Who's there?

Nun

Nun who?

Nun of your business!

Knock, knock.

Who's there?

Needle!

Needle who?

Needle little money for the movies!

Knock, knock.

Who's there?

Needle.

Needle who?

Needle little help gettin' in the door.

Knock, knock.

Who's there?

A little old lady.

A little old lady who?

I didn't know you could yodel.

Knock, knock.

Who's there?

Police

Police who?

Police may I come in?

Knock, knock.

Who's there?

Police.

Police who?

Police hurry—I'm freezing out here!

Knock, knock.

Who's there?

Police!

Police who?

Police let us in, it's raining outside!

Knock, knock.

Who's there?

Scold.

Scold who?

Scold outside—let me in!

Will you remember me in 2 minutes?

Yes.

Knock, knock.

Who's there?

Hey, you didn't remember me!

Knock, knock.

Who's there?

Tank

Tank who?

You're welcome!

Knock, knock.

Who's there?

Figs

Figs who?

Figs the doorbell, it's broken!

Knock, knock.

Who's there?

Water

Water who?

Water you doing in my house?

Knock, knock.

Who's there?

Who!

Who who?

That's what an owl says!

Knock, knock.

Who's there?

Wooden shoe

Wooden shoe who?

Wooden shoe like to hear another joke?

Knock, knock.

Who's there?

Sherwood

Sherwood Who?

Sherwood like you to open the door!

Knock, knock.

Who's there?

Cow-go

Cow-go who?

No, Cow go MOO!

Knock, knock.

Who's there?

Kiwi

Kiwi who?

Kiwi go to the store?

Knock, knock.

Who's there?

Noah!

Noah who?

Noah good place to get something to eat?

Knock, knock.

Who's there?

Abby!

Abby who?

Abby birthday to you!

Knock, knock.

Who's there?

Who

Who, who?

Are you an owl?

Knock, knock.

Who's there?

Radio!

Radio who?

Radi-o-not, here I come!

Knock, knock.

Who's there?

Repeat

Repeat who?

Who, who, who

Knock, knock.

Who's there?

Luke.

Luke who?

Luke through the keyhole to see!

Knock, knock.

Who's there?

Cash

Cash who?

I knew you were a nut!

Knock, knock.

Who's there?

Boo!

Boo who?

I didn't mean to make you cry!

Knock, knock.

Who's there?

Olive!

Olive who?

Olive you!

Knock, knock.

Who's there?

Mikey!

Mikey who?

Mikey doesn't fit in the keyhole!

Knock, knock.

Who's there?

Ya!

Ya Who?

What are you so excited about?

Knock, knock.

Who's there?

Door

Door who?

Do-your homework!

Knock, knock.

Who's there?

Elmo!

Elmo who?

You don't know who Elmo is?

Knock, knock.

Who's there?

Broken pencil!

Broken pencil who?

Never mind, it's pointless!

Knock, knock.

Who's there?

I am!

I am who?

You don't know who you are?

Knock, knock.

Who's there?

Utah!

Utah who?

Utah-king to me?

Knock, knock.

Who's there?

Rida

Rida who?

Rida lot of books!

Knock, knock.

Who's there?

Tiss!

Tiss who?

A Tiss-who is good for blowing your nose!

Knock, knock.

Who's there?

Yodel-lay-he!

Yodel-lay-he-who?

Yodel-lay-he-who,

I didn't know you can yodel!

Knock, knock.

Who's there?

B-9!

B-9 who?

B-9, I-17, N-32, G-41 O-74, I've got BINGO!

Knock, knock.

Who's there?

Double

Double who?

W!

Knock, knock.

Who's there?

Gorilla

Gorilla who?

Gorilla me a hamburger!

Knock, knock.

Who's there?

Ben and Jimmy

Ben and Jimmy who?

Ben down and Jimmy a kiss.

Knock, knock.

Who's there?

Clara

Clara who?

Clara space on the table!

Knock, knock.

Who's there?

For

For who?

For you!

Knock, knock.

Who's there?

Luvs

Luvs who?

Luvs you!

Knock, knock.

Who's there?

Your mom

Your mom who?

Your mom! Now open the door or you're grounded.

Knock, knock.

Who's there?

Cash

Cash who?

No thanks, I prefer peanuts!

Knock, knock.

Who's there?

Snow

Snow who?

Snowbody!

Knock, knock.

Who's there?

Shelby

Shelby who?

She'll be coming around the mountain!

Knock, knock.

Who's there?

Water

Water who?

Water you doing?

Knock, knock.

Who's there?

Dishes

Dishes who?

Dishes your friend!

Knock, knock.

Who's there?

Some bunny!

Some bunny who?

Some bunny has been eating all my carrots!

Knock, knock.

Who's there?

Nacho

Nacho who?

Nacho momma!

Knock, knock.

Who's there?

Goat

Goat who?

Goat to the door and find out.

Knock, knock.

Who's there?

You know

You know who?

Avada Kadavra!

Knock, knock.

Who's there?

Silence

Silence who?

(Stay quiet)

Knock, knock.

Who's there?

Alfred

Alfred who?

Alfred the needle if you sew!

Knock, knock.

Who's there?

Sorry

Sorry who?

Sorry wrong door!

Knock, knock.

Who's there?

Claire

Claire who?

Claire out the room!

Knock, knock.

Who's There?

Barbie

Barbie Who?

Barbie Q Chicken!

Knock, knock.

Who's there?

Ash

Ash who?

Do you need a tissue?

Knock, knock.

Who's there?

Peas

Peas who?

Peas let me in now!

Knock, knock.

Who's there?

A herd.

A herd who?

A herd you were home, so I came over!

Knock, knock.

Who's there?

Ya. Ya Who?

Wow, I'm excited to see you too.

Knock, knock.

Who's there?

Boo!

Boo who?

Don't cry, it's just me.

Knock, knock.

Who's there?

Interrupting pirate!

Interrup… ARRRRRRRRR!

Knock, knock.

Who's there?

Issac!

Issac who?

Issac of knock, knock jokes already!

Printed in Great Britain
by Amazon